South American Animals

Poison Dart Frogs

ABDO
Publishing Company

Big Buddy BOOKS
South American Animals

by Julie Murray

VISIT US AT
www.abdopublishing.com

Published by ABDO Publishing Company, PO Box 398166, Minneapolis, Minnesota 55439.

Printed in the United States of America, North Mankato, Minnesota.
092013
012014

 PRINTED ON RECYCLED PAPER

Coordinating Series Editor: Rochelle Baltzer
Editor: Marcia Zappa
Contributing Editors: Megan M. Gunderson, Bridget O'Brien, Sarah Tieck
Graphic Design: Maria Hosley
Cover Photograph: *iStockphoto*: ©iStockphoto.com/kikkerdirk.
Interior Photographs/Illustrations: *Getty Images*: O. Louis Mazzatenta (p. 11), Margarette Mead (p. 19), Mark Moffett (p. 27); *Glow Images*: Glenn Bartley (p. 29), © Tom Brakefield/CORBIS (p. 7), Dietmar Heinz (p. 13), Ivan Kuzmin (p. 15), ARCO / Wittek, R. (p. 5); *iStockphoto*: ©iStockphoto.com/kikkerdirk (p. 25), ©iStockphoto.com/CarlosEduardoRamirez (p. 9), ©iStockphoto.com/JohanSjolander (p. 4); *Minden Pictures*: © Michael & Patricia Fogden (p. 13), © Pete Oxford/NPL (p. 23); *Science Source*: Jacques Jangoux (p. 9), Martin Shields (p. 16), Mark Smith (p. 17); *Shutterstock*: Ammit Jack (p. 4), Anneka (p. 21), Pablo H Caridad (p. 9), Asaf Eliason (p. 10), Dr. Morley Read (p. 8), worldswildlifewonders (p. 17).

Library of Congress Cataloging-in-Publication Data

Murray, Julie 1969-
  Poison dart frogs / Julie Murray.
    pages cm. -- (South American animals)
  ISBN 978-1-62403-192-2
1. Dendrobatidae--Juvenile literature. I. Title.
  QL668.E233M87 2014
  597.8'77--dc23
                    2013026907

Contents

Long ago, nearly all land on Earth was one big mass. About 200 million years ago, the land began to break into **continents**. One of these is South America.

Poison dart frogs are also called poison frogs and poison arrow frogs.

South America includes several countries and **cultures**. It is known for its rain forests and interesting animals. One of these animals is the poison dart frog.

Poison Dart Frog Territory

There are about 150 to 250 different types of poison dart frogs. They live in northern South America and Central America. Central America is the southern part of North America.

Poison dart frogs live in **tropical** rain forests. These forests are warm, wet, and thick with plants. Most types of poison dart frogs live near water, such as streams or ponds. Some live on mountains.

Poison Dart Frog Territory

Poison dart frogs live in areas with plenty of plants. These provide shade from the hot sun.

Welcome to South America!

If you took a trip to where poison dart frogs live, you might find…

S O U T H

P A

…tons of bugs.

South America is home to the world's largest tropical rain forest. The Amazon has more types of plants and animals than anywhere else. This includes up to 30 million different kinds of bugs! Many of these make good meals for poison dart frogs.

S O U

Strait of Magellan

Cape Horn

...ears of corn.

Corn (*below*) is one of the most common crops in South America. It is used to make arepas (*left*) and other foods. It is also used to make a drink called chicha.

...rainy days.

The Chocó area of Colombia is one of the wettest spots in the world. There, it rains more than 300 days each year!

Take a Closer Look

Poison dart frogs have small bodies. Adults are only 0.4 to 2.6 inches (1 to 6.6 cm) long. Their thin legs are strong and built for jumping and climbing. Their toes have round tips that help them hold on to leaves.

A poison dart frog has large eyes on the sides of its face. It has two small **nostrils** and a wide mouth.

Poison dart frogs weigh less than one ounce (28 g). That is about the weight of five quarters.

Danger!

Poison dart frogs are famous for their poisonous skin. Not all types of these frogs are toxic. But, many have poison that can cause swelling, sickness, **paralysis**, and even death.

The golden poison dart frog is the most toxic. Scientists believe just one has enough poison to kill ten grown men!

The golden poison dart frog has only one predator. It is a snake that is not bothered by the frog's poison.

The golden poison dart frog is one of the most toxic animals on Earth.

Uncovered!
For hundreds of years, native people in Colombia have used poison dart frog poison. They coat their darts in it for hunting. This is how the frogs got their name.

Scientists believe that poison dart frogs don't make their poison. Instead, they get it from the food they eat.

The frogs eat bugs that feed on poisonous plants. The poison passes from the bugs to the frogs. Then, it is let out through their skin.

Poison dart frogs that live in zoos or as pets are not poisonous. That is because they eat different foods than wild frogs.

A Beautiful Warning

Most poison dart frogs are brightly colored. They may be green, yellow, orange, red, blue, or several colors together.

A poison dart frog's bright skin tells predators that it is toxic. This keeps the frog safe because predators stay away!

Uncovered!
Other animals use bright colors or stripes to keep predators away. These include monarch butterflies and skunks.

Yellow-banded poison dart frogs are black with a yellow pattern.

Strawberry poison dart frogs are generally bright red with blue legs.

Poison dart frogs that aren't poisonous are generally dull brown and good at hiding.

A Frog's Life

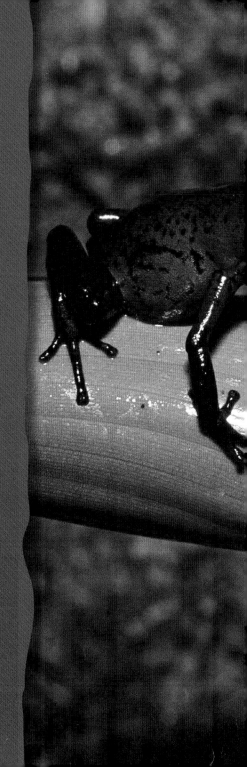

Poison dart frogs are active during the day. Most live on the forest floor. Some types live high in trees.

Some poison dart frogs live alone. Others live in pairs or small groups. Poison dart frogs meet as they claim home areas and choose **mates**. Sometimes, they come together to care for their young.

A group of frogs is called an army.

Uncovered!
Adult poison dart frogs are not good at swimming. They rarely go in water.

Mealtime

Poison dart frogs eat many different types of bugs. These include ants, termites, beetles, flies, and crickets. A frog captures its meal using its long, sticky tongue.

Poison dart frogs use their strong eyesight to find bugs.

Incredible Eggs

Poison dart frogs are **amphibians**. A female lays up to 50 eggs. She usually chooses a spot that is wet, dark, and quiet. This may be under a leaf or rock.

One or both parents care for the eggs. They keep them clean, wet, and safe. After two to four weeks, the eggs **hatch**.

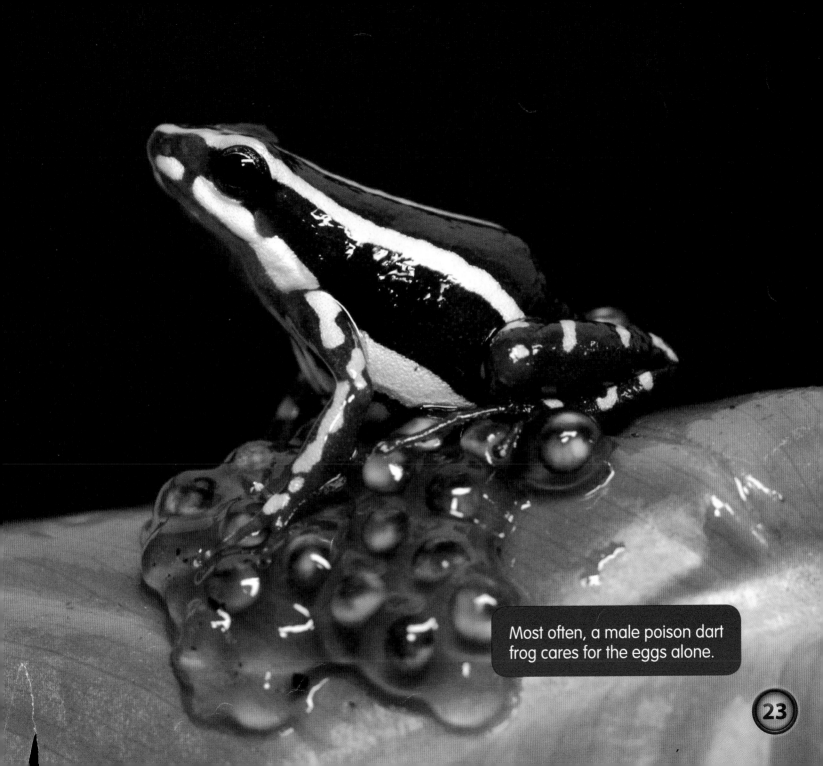

Most often, a male poison dart frog cares for the eggs alone.

Tadpoles

Parents carry their tadpoles to little ponds, streams, and other places that collect water. These include coconut shells and the center of plants.

Poison dart frogs **hatch** as tadpoles. Tadpoles have tails for swimming. And, they have gills for breathing underwater. The tadpoles swim onto the back of one of their parents. The parent carries them to water, where they can grow.

Uncovered!

Some types of poison dart frog tadpoles eat their brothers and sisters! So, their parents must take each tadpole to its own spot.

As tadpoles grow, they begin to change into frogs. This change is called metamorphosis (meh-tuh-MAWR-fuh-suhs). It takes 6 to 14 weeks.

Over time, the gills are replaced with **lungs**. The tadpole grows legs and loses its tail. And, its mouth changes so it can catch bugs.

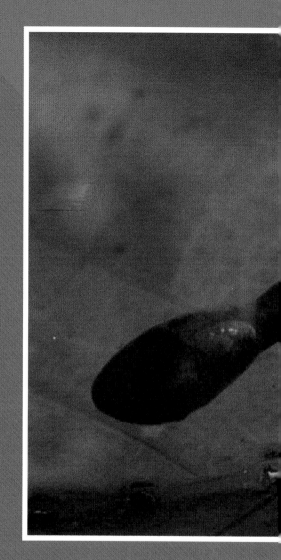

Many tadpoles are left on their own. Yet others get help from their parents. For example, some mothers lay special eggs for their tadpoles to eat.

27

Survivors

Life in South America isn't easy for poison dart frogs. New buildings and farms take over their **habitats**. And because of their bright colors, people often capture them to sell as pets.

Still, these frogs **survive**. People work to save their rain forest homes. Poison dart frogs help make South America an amazing place.

In the wild, poison dart frogs live for up to 15 years.

Wow!

I'll bet you never knew...

...that poison can be good! Scientists are searching for ways to use the poison dart frog's poison. They think it may help people with pain, heart problems, and blood problems.

...that poison dart frogs aren't the only tiny, bright, toxic frogs in the world. Very similar frogs live in Madagascar. But, they are not related to poison dart frogs.

...that the poison dart frog family's scientific name means "tree walker."

Important Words

amphibian (am-FIH-bee-uhn) an animal that lives part of its life in water and part of its life on land.

continent one of Earth's seven main land areas.

culture (KUHL-chuhr) the arts, beliefs, and ways of life of a group of people.

habitat a place where a living thing is naturally found.

hatch to be born from an egg.

lungs body parts that help the body breathe.

mate a partner to join with in order to reproduce, or have babies.

nostril an opening of a nose.

paralysis (puh-RA-luh-suhs) a loss of the power to move or feel part of the body.

survive to continue to live or exist.

tropical of or relating to parts of the world where temperatures are warm and the air is moist all the time.

Web Sites

To learn more about poison dart frogs, visit ABDO Publishing Company online. Web sites about poison dart frogs are featured on our Book Links page. These links are routinely monitored and updated to provide the most current information available.

www.abdopublishing.com

Index